From The Trenches of Korea to the Trench in Mission Control

An oral history of the life and times of
John S. Llewellyn

*Exact transcriptions of oral recordings
of John Llewellyn made by*

Maureen Bowen
Todd Johnston

4

I was born in 1931 near Tidewater, Virginia, very close to Yorktown in a place called Dare. A lot of stuff was happening in that period, especially in the world of politics. Nazi Germany was beginning. Also a major step in science was the publishing of the theory of Relativity. And in 1935, something called Quantum Mechanics was postulated by a guy named Erwin Schrodinger who wrote what was called The Wave Equation.

My Daddy had just gotten out of the United States Navy and was working near Washington, DC. It was tough to find something to do. When Daddy was in the Navy, he was a member of the 'Black Gang'. They were the ones that shoveled coal into the burners of the ship's steam engines. That was before they went to diesel. Most of the Navies had coal. You could always tell because of black smoke coming from their stacks. My Mother was teaching High School in Arlington, VA. When he married my Mother he found a steady job with The Swift Company as a meat packer. He got really strong lifting all those carcasses because that's how they got them out of the refrigerator cars. That was a really tough bunch. They could take those steers and put them on their backs and walk, dump them and start working on them. He may also have had what is known today as post traumatic stress disorder (PTSD). My Daddy was manic when he worked. He read a lot of history and knew it well. He also knew the Bible. He could carry on long discussions about all kinds of topics. I knew him well because I came from the days when your father and you worked together from sun up to sun down. He was a fisherman and a truck farmer. We used to raise vegetables, put them on a train or hauled them into town on our trailer. That's how we made a living. It was very hard work. We still had mules and horses in those days. I happened to be one of the boys that knew how to plow. Not everybody could plow a field but I was one guy who could do it. Which made me have a set job. It's kind of my thing to do in life. "I plowed many fields."

It was a time when southern civilization was in a state of decay. They had a lot of Civil War veterans there, they had a lot of women that were born and had lived like my Grandmother who was born in Charles City County at a place called Sunnyside. She lived during the siege of Richmond and she never forgot it. Her brother left because her Father told him to get his ass out of Richmond. He was about seventeen or something. My Great Grandmother, was married to my Great Grandaddy who fought in the Civil War. He had all these books in his library called "Lee's Lieutenants."

When I was in Newport News, VA, on very rainy days I used to go to her house and read all that stuff. She had a great library so I was really lucky to have that kind of intellectual stimulation that most people didn't have around them. It was part of the kind of culture I came from because the old Southern way of life was still very much alive there.

I had a very talented brother, Charles. As he grew up, he became more of an artist and stuff like that. He was really bright and he was huge. I'll never forget that. I spent most of my life wearing his clothes. When I came along, you always wore your brother's clothes which made me mad . He grew to about 6' 3" and he was very well built and a good athlete too. He still holds the record for the High School discus in the state of Virginia. We played Football together. We did all that. And he was a very unusual…in fact, when we were on the track team, they said one time the Llewellyn brothers beat York (rival school), because when I ran and he threw a shot and the discus we had enough points between us to beat a whole school. I used to run 100's and 440's. It was good for me. In 1946 I could run a 10:00 flat hundred. There was only one guy from Houston who could run faster than me. He ran a 9:06 hundred in High School.

I started playing football because my mother and my grandmother decided that going to school in York County was not the place I was going to learn anything. So I went to Newport News High School. Nobody understood my brother Charles and me. Because we were from York-town we would take our shoes off to walk to school. We did all kinds of things because we didn't have organized sports. Baseball had different leagues. They had the Scouts instead of baseball teams and they had different organizations that boys played in. Everybody I knew was in some kind of sandlot team as we called it. Even the men played it. And everybody used to play football. Dr. Kraft used to play baseball for one of the sandlot teams. That's how I met him for the first time. I think he stepped on my foot. Those days it was so different playing High School baseball, semi-pro they called it. Newport News High School was a really good school. We had a really good staff and all these teachers had been around a long time. In fact some of the teachers I had, went to school with my mother at the State Teachers College.

Growing up I'd listen to my Daddy while we were working. (I remember I did all the spraying and Charles did all the pumping) . I'd be spraying the apple trees and my Daddy used to say to me, remember this John, that revenge is sweet. That's what he said. He told me things like this over and over again. He used to say "Give no quarter and ask no quarter." And for some reason, that got in my mind. It had a really interesting effect on me. I got to a point I was running around fighting all the time. It seemed like…because even in those days the people from different High Schools always had a tough guy that was coming down and whipped somebody in Newport News. In fact, when I went to Stanton (military school), the thing I missed most I told them was that I couldn't wait to get home to have a good fight. These guys up there couldn't fight worth a damn.

Stanton was a Military Academy. They sent me up there because I had an appointment at the Naval Academy. I would have been in the class of '54. But by the time the Korean War came along, I was called into the Marine Reserves. I went into the Marine Reserves after a movie called 'Sands of Iwo Jima' came out. I think everybody I knew was in the Marines. In fact, most of us in Korea that made up the major part of a military operation were all young kids. We were lucky to have officers and non-commissioned officers from World War II that told us what to do. And it couldn't have been any better because a boy seventeen years old is probably the best Marine you're ever going to get because he doesn't give a [darn]. He doesn't have any idea why he's there or what he's doing. In fact, when I joined the Marine Corps, *I thought I would be fighting Yankees*. I actually thought that's who I was going to fight. That's how sad it was. I didn't know where Korea was. My Daddy used to say it was "Over yonder." I didn't even know what Asia was.

The Korean War started in 1950 when the North Koreans penetrated as far south as Pusan, crossing the line we called the 38th parallel.

Running Away from Home

When I was thirteen I started changing my birthday around. I got to the point I didn't know even when I was born. It could have been from '31 to '33 but anyway, I never did know. I went to get my cattleman's papers right after World War II and because of a change in mechanization of farms, they did away with thousands of mules and good horses. We had some of the best livestock and cows. They sent them to Europe as a part of the program to reestablish the European nations with farm interests. We sent all that stuff over there. They [the military] had what you call a 'cattleman'. I joined the civilian Navy [maritime] and became a 'cattleman'.

I picked up a cattle boat in Newport News because it was such a busy port. In fact, they'd become the port of embarkation for World War II which gave it a completely different status of any other state seaport. The cattle boat was going to Italy. I got on it and the cook was queer. He tried to ['come on to me'] me all the way to Brooklyn. I'll never forget the night before we left. I spent all night running around the tables inside the galley. Soon as I got there I jumped ship, borrowed some money and called my Daddy, told him to send me a bus ticket. That's what he did. I came home very much changed. I was never the same. I mean, High School was nothing to me. I couldn't believe how dumb everybody was.

I always took a risk every time I had a (I used to say) a fork in the road, I'd always take…I'd look at the directions I might go. If it says becoming a cattleman is a neat thing and I need that experience. Why do you need to stay in High School? Because I used to go there and watch the ships go every day and make up like I was on one of them. It was really a neat place to live in those days.

I happened to be part of a culture that they sent boys to military schools [Stanton]. That was the best thing to do because they weren't going to jail. I had had all this stuff going on, and I was becoming some kind of…I don't know...person that was not capable of staying in High School. So I went up there and I loved it because it was military, and I loved the football there. Not a lot of the football players were that intellectual in those days. In those days if you were a football player, you played the whole game if you were on first string. And you had to take stuff besides Social Sciences, real courses like Engineering, Legal, Pre-Law, History, much of the stuff that was taught in colleges. Stanton was a Prep School for the Academy. And then when the thing (Korea) started I heard they were calling the Reserves up. I jumped out my window and got a ride to Newport News and joined the reserves.

The Marines

My Mother went ape. She told me not to do it because she didn't want me to join. I said it was a good deal 'cause I was gonna' get drafted anyway. In fact, I actually marched down Washington Avenue to the train station as a Marine Reserve, and got on the train and left town like they did during the Civil War. I met Marines - especially ones from New York and up North. They had no idea how we operated in the South. It was a real disconnect.

I'll never forget the night we went to Paris Island on the train. The guys from New York were scared to death. Can you imagine knowing some of those guys had never seen dirt? They grew up in Brooklyn and places like that. They were always on concrete. Then they started in the Marines. No wonder so many of them got messed up. They didn't even know what a swamp was. They had to walk through it all.

Private John S. Llewellyn
2ⁿᵈ rank far left column

So now I was in the Marine Corps, yeah. That was perfect for me. I was so glad to be a Marine. I didn't have to go to school anymore. I was going through Boot Camp. I was so proud to be there, in fact, because I'd gone through Stanton, I knew how to take an M1 apart. And I could do that in a New York minute. That made me kind of an interesting guy to have in Boot camp because I also knew a lot of military structures we had learned in those little books they gave us to read. I knew a lot of that even before I went there. So I was an outstanding member. But then I ran into trouble, because I was a Southerner, and the guy that was our drill instructor was from Pennsylvania. He made us jump in the fire barrels* and sing Dixie every [damn] morning. I guess because he really didn't particularly like what he was doing.

*Fire barrels were put around the tents and filled with water in case the tents burned down. The water was very cold.

Korea

One morning I went by the Gunnery Sergeant's office. I said, "I want to come in here and tell you I want to go to Korea." I don't want to go to that school. He said, "I can't send you to Korea. That's like saying you're going to die." I said, that's why I joined the Marine Corps. Next thing we had this big argument. He ended up putting me on the draft to go to Korea. I wanted to go. A lot of times after that, I wonder why I did that. But I always did stuff like that.

I joined up with the First Marine Division and went over with an early group of guys that did all the first wave stuff like Inchon [reservoir] and the trap. All the early stuff that the Marines did. It was an incredible experience.

I was with the Fifth Marines Able Company and we had hit Red Beach. We actually had to go on the beach and the tides fell by twenty feet and we got in there late. So we had these ladders, we had to use to limb over the sea wall at Inchon (September 15, 1950).

I was about the third guy. You can see me on the ladder with my machine gun on my shoulder. You can see the Platoon Sergeant before me and as soon as he walked over the wall he caught one

I never got over that. He was a Mexican.* He was one of the first guys that got killed in the Korean War.

*Medal of Honor posthumously awarded to 1st Lt Baldomero Lopez 15 September 1950. Ref: Korean battle chronology: unit-by-unit United States casualty figures by Richard Eker

The North Koreans didn't have any idea we were going to do that. They were down south in the Pusan perimeter. The whole North Korean army was down there. We had not a bad landing because they didn't have any way to get people in to stop us. Our submarines also hit Blue Beach, but it turned out they waited so long that they had to walk in through the mud. It's been said that Inchon was a smart thing to do. Various men were credited for it, but when you think of what we went through just to get ashore, I wonder. We would start at Inchon and move up the road towards Seoul. And that's where we had our next objective. Right outside of Seoul is a hill called 206 where we got bogged down. It was some of the heaviest fighting we'd ever done.

The primary reason we went into Inchon I've been reminded, was that it was a really good way to trap all the North Koreans down South because everything was down around a place called the Pusan perimeter.

It was General Douglas MacArthur's idea and he argued for it but nobody would listen to him at first. Even the Marines said they didn't want to do it because they didn't have enough trained people but ['Doug'] kept arguing until we did it.

We had a lot of Americans at Inchon and The Navy had them up there too. They were very aware of the tides and the problems, and they were the ones that could almost set the dates of the tides. They were there when it happened.

We immediately set up sites because that was necessary. Strategically, Seoul was in a good place because it had the Imjin River running through it that went to the China Sea. Like all rivers that aren't dammed it was mostly swamps. Strategically it was a real edge with all the stuff going North. It was also the Capital of Korea. Syngman Rhee was there.

We entered Seoul about two weeks later after a big battle for the high ground on the outside of Seoul. I think it was [hill] 609. It took us a long time to get done with that. It was really a bitter battle. It's actually one of the toughest ones I can remember, even tougher than the problem with the Chosin Reservoir, except that was so cold. And there were so many Chinese.

Able Company had point going through Seoul. It took us a long time to get through. We really did a good job on it.

We brought artillery in, lined 'em up, and fired canister shot all the way to the railroad station. We just blew up Seoul right through the middle. They had their major defense set up around the railroad station. It was a good place because it was the only place you had stuff like a fort. You had cement. You had all those rail cars. It was a place like a castle really. You had to go through those things to get inside of the perimeter. That was really something. We did that with tanks and stuff. Just blew the whole thing down. I'll never forget that.

It took two weeks to secure Seoul and then we immediately started training again to get our ranks rebuilt before we went North. Nobody believed we were going to do it. We had the whole army from the East Coast through all that punchbowl area. We had the whole 10th Corps, they called it. Anyway we deployed toward the north sometime in November on the Marine Corps birthday.

The Army brought in their people to hold that line we had secured in

Seoul. I think it was called the Kansas line. The Marines were on a major push to Indochina and our Marine Generals were very upset with it. We were capturing Chinese… we even got overrun with them and sometimes we had more Chinese captured than we had Marines. That's a very bad situation to be in because you have to stand 100% watch. You look one way and you've still got to keep looking the other way. It was a lot of strain on us.

Chosin Reservoir

It was high altitude. We were like up around 10,000 feet and it was extremely cold. That winter that came in was one of the worst winters for a long time. It came out of Mongolia. It was very cold and the ones that suffered more than we did were the Chinese. I couldn't believe the number of frozen feet. You could just look at their tennis shoes-their whole foot would be frozen. They lost so many people, not only to the Marines…but to the weather. We had learned in World War II about kamikaze attacks where you would actually get overrun. You would hold your position…and they had so many that they were able to get through you. We had developed all kinds of tactics for that. Fields of fire were put in by the guy who knew something about it. And that's what we did for about two days. We had a real good line. We had two battalions up front and one battalion in the back. The battalion in the back was in Koto-ri and that was where Col Chesty Puller was. And that was a main place to hold. That's where all the roads came back to Koto-ri. There's a rail line there and they also had an airstrip where they took out our wounded. The Air Force had C47's and C46's. Koto-ri is where we retreated after we got overrun along the Chosin Reservoir.

We had the high ground. We must have been up at 9-10,000 feet because it was so cold I could tell that it hurt to breathe. And we had had a good meal for Thanksgiving. It was really neat. We had all kinds of good food like real turkey and cranberry out in the middle of this god awful place, and we were just so happy. As soon as we finished that, we started building a MLR, they called it a Main Line of Resistance around the top of this mountain. I forget the name of the mountain. That was the total 5th Marine Regiment. Two battalions on the hill. 1st and 2nd battalion was on the hill and then they had another battalion back near where Col. Chesty Puller was to protect the Headquarters. We had two of them, two back battalions. The thing those guys could do in that type of tactical situation – you would actually protect your Headquarters. Because they had all the stuff they needed to keep from being overrun and they usually had enough time to know what was happening. And they had another battalion there to stop them. What happened was, the bad thing that happened…the Chinese were able to get through that battalion's roadblock and brought tanks in. It was hard for us to stop them. We were cut in two from Chesty for almost a week.

We got overrun because the Chinese came to us all the way up the mountain. The Chinese had been able to penetrate our roadblock. Actually, we didn't have a complete line from the first battalion. I was using a machine gun. I was a machine gunner, even though I started off as ammo carrier that night, I got to be a gunner. I stayed gunner for a long time…that was lucky.

The Chinese…their bugles…I could see them coming. I saw them when they stopped all their running around in circles like ants down there. I couldn't believe there were that many people. And I just looked at it. I never saw anything like it in my life. I was from Dare, Virginia. The only city I'd ever gone to was Washington, DC and Richmond. I didn't have any idea. I thought Chinese ran restaurants. Anyway, that's when I dragged a case of grenades to my hole…had a whole case of them that they brought up where ammo was stored and stuff. That's why I went back I got a bunch 'cause I had kind of strategic position.… the gun was there on port…I was on the flank. This little ravine went up between me and the gun.

I was sent there to stop that fight. That's what I was put there for. And when they first started, I knew they were around with their bugles. And then I could see…I thought I saw one. All he did was jump in the snow. All I could see was the wind blowing. I said was that a Chinese or not? I threw a grenade right in the middle of it. And when I did, there was a whole bunch in there. They had gotten that close to me. But it really turned out right, I had so many grenades, I just started throwing them. I had almost a little artillery attack going. I thought I wiped them all out 'cause they were down in this thing [hole]. And that's when it started. Then the machine guns started firing and I could see all of these flares going off and see how many there were. Everywhere you saw the light lit up they were there. Some of them had white tops on. You couldn't see them. That's good camouflage, having white coats and dark pants. They looked like trees running around. It was really something and I watched that.

Yes it was. In fact, I was already up there setting the fire piece on the gun…the machine gun, 'cause I had to change a barrel in the middle of it. We'd burned the barrel out. The tracers were going on and you could see them doing helixes. I had a gun barrel and I knew where it was, and I went and got it. I put the new barrel in it.

They [Chinese] expected us to get overrun. They didn't expect us to fold up. And what happened, the Chinese… were so many of them…it was really funny, especially in this situation, the snow and all, that they didn't know where the line was. The Chinese, there were so many of them, they got to a point, they didn't even know where the gun was firing from. I had my K-BAR and I put the fire piece on my machine gun. Then I heard this click go off. It was a Sub-Thompson. A Chinese had had me [in his sights]with a brand new Sub-Thompson. I never looked at it. I said where did he get that from? Remember, the Chinese we were fighting were part of Chiang Kai-Shek's army, that's where he got it. They killed so many of them, that China put them out in the outback and they never came back to tell their stories. It's incredible how they could do that. But anyway, I heard that later. I had this K-Bar and all I did was stab him with it because I didn't have anything else. I actually stabbed him with it. He didn't have any rounds left in his Sub-Thompson. He probably got excited in cold weather and he couldn't find another magazine. He fell down in the trench on top of me. For the rest of the night, hearing the Chinese running by my trench, I laid there with this Chinese soldier. I didn't want to make any noise because I thought he'd holler at some of them coming by me. I didn't know if he was dead or not. He was laying on top of me and I laid there and I said, this has got to be a horrible way to die. I couldn't believe it. I could hear them…the Chinese by this time were just coming by in tennis shoes making tracks. Nobody was shooting anymore. I said man…that was a sign. You heard it for a long time, must have been an hour of them running by. I looked and there was nothing left of our area. It was all bodies and even the Marines were gone. So I sat there and I was afraid to make coffee because I didn't want to light my little stove. I sat there in the cold. Finally I heard the Gunnery Sergeant calling, Reveille, everybody get up! And no kidding, the guys were coming out of the holes. We must have had thirty or forty people left. They all did what I did. We never said anything about it. The Sergeant said, "Come up here, we're going to reorganize and go after them." I said, "you are crazy." I can't believe it. He said we're going in and coming up from behind them. He says, "we'll get a bunch of them that way." I thought to myself, if they're anything like me, they won't be able to shoot. I couldn't believe it. He got up like he had a white board and he started drawing pictures in the snow. "Here we are, here's the battalion." I don't know how he knew they were in trouble, but "we gotta go help them out, and we got enough guys here to turn the battle. We'll come in behind them." I asked him "how long did you hear them?" I said there was an hour of hoof marks over at my place. I said, "Do you know how many [Chinese] that is? And we're going to go out there with this weeded out bunch of Marines that don't even know where they are?" Everybody had this real stare...I could see them. They had a thousand yard stare.

We actually took off and followed the tracks. By morning it was a clear day...it was crystal clear, a bluebird day. The Navy Corsairs could see the Chinese going up the hills and they just started on them. They just wiped them out. In fact, we got our M1's and everybody in the battalion, even the cooks and bakers got out and shot them. They [Chinese] turned and they just didn't know what to do. The Chinese officers led them right by us. God they lost a lot. I can't believe it.

I didn't have much ammo for my machine gun. It was hard to take the gun and the tripod, and the ammo. I was so tired anyway. A box of 30 ought 6 machine gun ammo weighs about nine pounds.

There were a lot of [reinforcements] that had tried to get to us to keep the casualties down. The British commandos out of Seoul tried to get up through there. Most of them were killed so they couldn't relieve the columns. It was a hard battle to Koto-ri, but we came out with everything, trucks, tents, and all of our dead.

It took us three days to get to Koto-ri. We fought the whole way. We

Koto-ri

were always in one of these [positions] where the flanks would run into problems and then we had the point. The point couldn't move and since we'd taken casualties anyway, they brought up a regiment of guys from the 7th Marines [to help bring us out]. We let them rest and they could use the latrines and stuff like that because they had the trucks with them. And they had some toilets. It was good to have them because we really couldn't relieve ourselves. You couldn't. At 40 below, if you exposed yourself, you would go into hypothermia.

Luckily we didn't eat much until we got somewhere. I never had a warm up tent to go into. I couldn't even clean my weapon. I was thinking about that. Then we got to Koto-ri, we had all the warm up tents and we could clean up a little bit. And that's where 'Chesty' had stopped them [Chinese]. We didn't have much trouble with them. There were so many that we killed and we got through that and got evacuated, our dead and wounded.

'Chesty' had brought his 105's out again and played the Civil War. Lined them up wheel to wheel. He shot canisters right in the middle. He just ruined them. You couldn't believe how many dead guys there were. I'll never forget when we moved out of there that the ice was melting and all these buried Chinese that had been napalmed and then froze. It was the weirdest picture to see all those dead Chinese frozen and the snow coming off of them. I thought to myself, what a weird thing. It kind of got me again, you know? I've seen a lot of nasty stuff in my life but it's a whole field of [dead people]. They looked like pine trees that you'd cut down, half way up.

Loading the fallen

The Corsairs caught up with the waves that were coming after us. You could see them coming back down. And their officers didn't know what to do. Yeah. They just let them walk in straight lines. I couldn't believe it. It was so easy to kill them. I guess they were demoralized too. That must have been a hell of a thing to lose that many people. Good God. It's almost hard to describe what happened. The next thing I knew, they were right in front of us, walking straight down a snow filled ravine, probably like 400 yards away. They were well within M1 shooting range. And with our marksmanship, I think everybody's shot got one. It went on for two hours.

When they were passing, we didn't get them all. I mean, there were still some that somebody else probably got. By this time Howard and George Companies had connected with a heroic battle that connected the hole in the line and we could actually make a withdrawal that was not erratic. We started going back, but we had to go back and pack all our gear in the trucks. We took the trucks with the dead and all our guns and ammo and we walked mountain roads to get out of there.

We actually put guards out and up front. In fact, we (5th Marines) were the point going out. Anytime something militarily would happen, we were usually the first ones that saw it. We would call up the other regiments to come up and clean out these pockets of Chinese that were on the outside. That's something we did when we walked down a road. -We always had our flanks up. That saved our lives. That's what the Army didn't do.

I'll never forget we were coming into Koto-ri and the 1st Marines there had built fires for us. That's where we stopped for the first time in a long time. The guys there were asking how come the wounded are walking and all those other guys are sitting in the trucks. We told them because they're all dead. I mean it's funny but it's not. The dead guys were frozen in the truck and the guy who asked the question couldn't tell. I never thought of that, but that was strange watching that. In fact, the air force didn't want to fly the dead out. We told them if they didn't do it, none of them would get out of there. Every pilot would be shot. We got every dead guy out of there. 'Chesty' made sure the pilots took every dead guy out of there.

From Koto-ri we went to Wonsan to evacuate. [Along the way] we had to build a bridge, like a railroad bridge from one point to the other. It was a Bailey bridge and the Marines had never done it. The Air Force dropped this and they also told us how to do it. And we did it. We had gotten guys all the way down the valley on the other side to hold off the Chinese while we built it. It was crazy. I actually indeed couldn't believe that. I said, "I can't believe this." It's in the books, though. We actually built that bridge in two days. We'd have never gotten out if we hadn't.

And the good thing was it was just another day. You know, you got so used to it you always said, who ordered this? When this bridge came up, it was just another day and I just knew it was going to happen. I guess that's where I got that stamina. You never gave up. You gotta' have that burning light of courage and know you'll do it. (Guerre -French?) You did it cause you're American. That's why we did it. We didn't do it for any other reason. It's hard for guys to say that, but most Marines, if you ask them, that's what they do it for. Most good pilots tell you, as f'd up as they are, will say, why'd you do that? Well I'm American, and that's why I did it. I'm proud of my country.

From there we went to Pusan. We started the retraining and we got re-placements. We had all these new guys. One of the things we did was to have football games between ourselves. I was on a football team and we won the championship. They gave us a silver cigarette case as a prize. That was our reward. These would hold Pall Malls which were long. Luckys would fall out of them. We carried them with us. It was such a deal to pull that thing out and pop it open and pull a Pall Mall that wasn't sweaty and brown. Because in our uniform we sweat so much, I never knew what a decent cigarette looked like.

Time came and they put us, each regiment, at a spot to go up and catch all the Chinese we could find between Pusan and Seoul. We went into places they where that had never seen white men before. The last time they saw anything like that it was the Japs. All that turned into be some kind of grab ass, because no matter what we did, we never caught them. We never spotted the person on the top of this mountain. We had him up there, but by the time we got to the top we didn't know where they were.

I had been moving up this hill, and what happened, I ran into a Chinese soldier in the trench line. I knew, they had been there. So I jumped down the trench. I was by myself, and I found a bunker. And because the Chineses knew exactly where the trench line was, they were throwing mortars in it. So I had to get out of there and I went into this Chinese bunker. It was real small so I couldn't take much in it. I went in there and I dropped my M1 rifle and I put it in the door. I was in there when I opened my new cigarette case. As I opened my brand new cigarette case, in the reflection behind me I saw this Chinese with a carbine. I just couldn't believe it. All I could do is swing around my trenching tool, I caught him on the side of the head. I could see where the truncheon tool went into his head, that's how I got out of that. That's the kind of things I just can't really believe…all that stuff that happened to me and I'm still living.

I checked his gun. He didn't have a round in it. It was one of those Russian carbines. I kept it. It was so pretty but they took it from me when I was getting ready to leave after I had hauled that damn thing around.

We caught a bunch of the Chinese in Ch'ongch'on which was an Air Base we actually flew into. It's funny. Ch'ongch'on was this big place where they had an airfield that was surrounded by mountains. My organization flew over the mountains and right down into Ch'ongch'on.

I thought the god damned place was already under the Marine's control. It wasn't. We got off the plane and they were shooting at us. We started the firefight right down on the runway. Just like they did when the Marines went into Hawaii. They did the same thing. They flew the airplanes into a field that the North Vietnamese had taken back. It took us a long time to get it back.

That went on for like two days. Because they had tanks and T-34's too we had to get rid of. It was kind of a place where you thought if you were a Chinese you would be safe because it was almost, like a caldera?

We were trying to push the North Koreans back north over the 38th parallel. They would have a field day with all their weapons and the civilian population was being highly abused. They had far superiority in numbers. They fought hard and they had their way with the villagers. We could see all those villages were kind of off limits anyway. That was a part of Korea that was under the hold of the chiefs and stuff. They had little pockets of Korea that didn't report to the Government. They were like warlords.

The combat we were involved in slowly wound down. They started the peace talks in Panmunjom, but the Chinese didn't want to sit at the table and end it but the UN wanted this thing ended. So, like they said, nobody's fighting anymore. We needed a show of strength, so they moved the Marines over to Panmunjom. Within two days we had had to burn a couple of villages and raised a lot of hell. The battlefield had gotten very messy as soon as we got there. Air strikes, bombardment, and Chinese in no-mans land. They had what you called a lot of OP's (outposts). You always had an outpost in no-mans land between your MLR's. That was a World War 1 tactic. We actually got back in World War 1, with trenches, an MLR with all kinds of barbed wire and concentrated mines and all that. And what UN did was they built a bunch of bleachers so everybody could watch the 5th Marines take back OP3. That's when I really got a lot of combat time in. That's the one where I got my Bronze Star.

I was on point. The Lieutenant at lead was arguing with the Battalion Commander. They said "pull your troops back." He said "I can't pull my troops back. We don't have control of the fire." They kept hollering back and forth and he said [forget] it, I'm going to attack." I listened to him and I said Jesus, I've been around this all my life. This is what Jackson told Lee at Antietam.

Before you'd withdraw you had to have the superiority of fire because otherwise it becomes a route. I actually got kind of turned on with it. I said, "let me go!" and he said, "you bet." He said, "take a couple of 45's too." I got the 45's off my gunners and I had four or five BARs (Browning Automatic Rifle). I didn't have a BAR bag or my magazines mounted either. I had these 45's and I could hardly walk up the hill with my pants not falling down. You know we had those big pockets. I can't believe it. I actually was one of the first guys at the trench line. There was nothing left. It turns out they had jumped off at the same time, 'cause I looked down the valley and I saw them all converged down in a corner. They had started their counter attack. In fact, it was deadly. They

**The Bronze Star citation
for Private First Class John S.**
Llewellyn reads:

"For heroic achievement in connection with operations against the enemy while serving as a machine gunner with a Marine infantry company in Korea on 9 May 1952. Private First Class Llewellyn was a member of a combat patrol which was brought under intense enemy artillery, mortar and small arms fire. When his machine gun was knocked out of action, he picked up the first available weapon, an automatic rifle, and continued the attack. Realizing that his platoon sergeant and all the squad leaders had become casualties, he unhesitatingly assumed the duties of platoon sergeant. Exposing himself to intense enemy fire with complete disregard for his own safety he encouraged and inspired the men of his unit, performing his own duties coolly and efficiently. His initiative and devotion to duty contributed materially to the successful withdrawal of the patrol. Private First Class LLEWELLYN'S heroic actions were in keeping with the highest traditions of the United States Naval Service."

actually almost wiped us out, they had so many of them. What I did was sit up there with my BAR and shoot down at them, hoping they weren't dropping more than forty yards away. With a BAR, I could set my sights and I was hoping I was getting a bunch of them. They didn't even know where it was coming from.

That's when I attacked the Chinese main thrust with what was left of the 1st Platoon. They didn't know what we were doing. They thought they were in a massive attack. We were right in the middle of shooting them. I killed so many of them at one time, I came running down off the hill and I ran into a bunch more. They were running at me, shooting and all that. There was a tank down in this valley and I ran straight to it. I jumped up on it and started to fire the 50 caliber at them. All these [Chinese] converged on our tank. But we had that 50 and it just ate them up. Once you start firing that thing, everybody wants to know, how can that work? You put a 50 on a jeep, you would think that the damn guy would get killed, but once you started shooting nobody can do anything about it. I mean what are you going to do, jump up with a burp gun and shoot out a 50? The bullets have explosive heads on them and when they go off, they will blow a guy in two. When you see that enough, you throw your burp gun down and run. And I'll never forget this Jewish guy who was a Corpsman. He got up on top to help me load and feed, and I had a runaway gun. You see, when you shoot so much, they start firing by themselves. You have to lift the top and twist the belt to make it quit firing. When I did that and pulled back on the cocking handle, it went off and blew part of his [genitals] away. That's so sad. He was just trying to help. I felt real bad.

I had been wounded in the legs and was sent to Japan and Yokohama Naval Base. That's where my knees got well. I wasn't even supposed to walk again, much less run. But I got to my Hospital ship and then went to Yokosuka where they had a great Navy Hospital. I recuperated there, and while I was there I got to go out. They cut a hole in the barbed wire fence so they could push me out in my wheelchair on nice and cold evenings. And I found out what a neat place that Yakuza was, those places and the [women] and stuff. So I got to be a real person. I had a chance to become part of the Armed Forces Police and I saw another nine months in Japan being a Policeman. I noticed how good the Japanese were as Police, and I found out, they could take a billy club and take a great big American down on the ground in minutes. I saw this great big white guy from places like Iowa or Texas. He hit a bull or a mule or oxen in front of this beer joint with his fist and knocked him down. He actually did it with his fist. And the Japanese police had him on the ground, begging. I said, I gotta learn how to do that.

So I went to Kano School of Judo in Japan. I was one of the only round eyes who went through the thing, so that's why I was pretty good at it. I stayed there about three months. And when the Korean situation started again, they transferred all of us that were in Japan, back to Korea. We all thought we were going to Hawaii. We heard rumors that the war was over and they would send you guys to Hawaii for the 3rd Marine Division which Chester Puller had started. What I did…I found out I was going to Korea…and I found out that I wasn't going with my own outfit in a rifle company. I said I wanted to go back with Able Company. They told me that I could. "You've already got enough Purple Hearts anyway, you can go get you another one." I said, "that suits me." That's what I did. I went back to my old outfit.

Back to School and NASA

I went to college in '54 about the time I got out of the Marines. I went to William and Mary first. Then when I got to work at [NASA] Langley. I was in the Physics and Math department there and I worked on Structures, that was the kind of the Queen of our Engineering in Langley, that's where all the smart guys were. I was over there with the Heat Transfer guys. I helped write CO3E (cobal programming language) which is a basic software for all the stuff we did after that. Bill Tindall developed that program, that's how I learned to know Bill. I wrote the re-entry equations with Bill Tindall, because I was the only guy who knew heat transfer. This is when people thought I was smart. I was probably one of their top guys at that time. I had a TR3, I was in college, I was Ivy League! I used to wear those grey suits with fanny pinchers, and those snap collars.

In fact, I had trouble being a Freshman and going through all that because I was so much different from the rest of the college people. I was 21 years old and most of them were 17. I was in the Freshman Dorm and they made so much hell in there one night, I got them all up and made them stand in front of the doors. I had these other crazy bastards that were Veterans with clipboards who were taking names and whipping ass. Then I took them on the blacktop and walked them around all night long and marched them. The President of the school got hold of me and said I should throw you out for this. You can't do that. I got all these Mothers up here. Why don't you use your influence for something else instead of doing that? That's when he scared me. Because I thought maybe I wasn't going to get to stay. -I had already started going to Graduate School at William and Mary to get my degree in Physics. I wanted to write a thesis on the boundary layer, you know, where the gas disassociates and becomes real hot because the stagnation temperatures. Stagnation temperatures were almost 10,000 degrees Fahrenheit. I worked for Max Faget in the Pilotless Aircraft Research Division (PARD). They were working on something to replace the Kamikazes. They were trying to build an unmanned airplane. That's where Kraft got in it. He knew all about Faget. Faget made the Blunt body. I worked for him the whole time when I was in college. When I got out, they sent me over to Structures. I got to know a lot of real good people in radiation and heat transfer. Then I went to the Space Task Group from because I knew Faget. He gave me my GS-9. Because of where I was at the time of the heating problems with the re-entry vehicles, I probably had more wind tunnel time than anybody at Langely.

That's where I met Glynn Lunney, when I was in the Space Task Group.

The Remote Tracking Sites

The thing the remote sites gave me was a good three or four months of learning telemetry and communication. I even had to learn Morse code. We had two card charts and had reduced the data, like you used to do for aircraft. You had to measure heat transfer coefficients and what was equivalent. That was really a lot of fun; that was perfect for me. I was the guy that was the boss of a remote site, because I was like an astronaut. I talked to the Cape. It was probably very similar to what was done at Bermuda. I had so much fun doing it. I found myself. It's the kind of thing that I'm so glad I ran into, because it gave a guy like me a way to really get into a really good engineering group called Flight Operations- it was perfect for me 'cause it was all real time and I loved it.

I did Zanzibar, the CSQ (Coastal Sentry Quebec, a tracking ship), Kano, Nigeria, and the Canary Islands. I was a Cap-Com (capsule communicator). In fact, I ran the CSQ because the ship Operations Officer had a nervous breakdown. We covered Shepard's flight from the CSQ. I covered the impact area. I was taken to the CSQ by a Navy Destroyer and 'high-lined from one ship to the other.

When the capsule went over I said "Main Shoot Deployed" or something like that that scared everybody. Kraft really got on my case about that. What is was, we had an antenna cable wrap problem and we lost all our telemetry which gave us erroneous information. He [Kraft] told me to come home and report to him. I reported on a Saturday morning; he had me in his office. He started asking where I had my training, and I told him. Then I said "I think you're over-reacting to this" which was NOT the right thing to say! I thought Llewellyn, you're not long for this job… here you are almost thirty years old in a dream job and you just told Kraft he over-reacted?[1]

After that I went to Kano, then to the site in the Canary Islands. I was at Canary Islands on MA-6*[2], Glenn's flight. We were the first ones that saw the indication that his heat shield was loose.

Then I was in Zanzibar and that's when I asked Kraft if I could call off the simulation as the local Mau-Maus were acting up. The King's African Rifles put up a perimeter around our site and they never got to us. I was very philosophical about it. At the end of my tour when I sent my Teletype status message I said, "Don't worry Chris, they got us surrounded. They're just where we want them."

We were such a prestigious operation, because Flight Dynamics actually argued with Astronauts. I knew I had the job I needed because I had to keep professional to keep a good status.

On my first mission from the Control Center we had Astronaut Scott

---

1 *He didn't fire me though and he even put me in his book "FLIGHT"*

2 *After Glenn's flight the world knew what NASA was doing, but most people had no idea what the controllers were doing. My brother worked at Langley and knew all about guidance and control but he knew nothing about real-time control.*

Carpenter who said nobody knew where he was. He was the one that thought he saw fireflies. I recall that his inverter was going off scale high and he wouldn't check it. He was completely outside his limits for Retrofire as he had run out of RCS fuel. After his chute deployed he was up above his parachutes. He had bounced around so much because he deployed something early. That's when I screamed in the Control Center. I think Kraft said he never saw anybody get as mad as I was. And Carl Huss was running around with his pencil making sure that we picked the right [retro] time. Oh yeah, we started that; that was really good. It started when we were down at the Cape. We had a really neat guy, a little short guy, named Clay Hicks who used to support us down there.

The other thing I did, was become an expert on clocks. There was some guy that built the Mercury clock. He was the best clock maker in the United States but it broke him because the thing wouldn't work. As it was, you could only update the Gemini clock with time to go. You couldn't load a time and then count it down. That became something I had to deal with for two or three years in Gemini because nobody ever set the right time.

The Simulations

As far as we were all concerned, the simulations were real. They were really more than a "Sim." We we're able to take a physical problem and turn it into a thought. Once you visualized it, you could develop really interesting abilities to make things seem so real based upon our experiences. That always amazed me. When you think about it, when you have an experience, then you can use it as a thought. Think about how important that is. Most everything we do, you have to make up something before you can examine it. If you ask me "John, how does a car work?", I have to actually visualize a car so that I can tell you.

I used to do a lot of work on Sunday whether I liked it or not. We'd get into all day Sunday sessions in a room, and for some reason, [Cliff] Charlesworth never did get tired. Only thing he never did was get hungry. He was perfect. It didn't matter how much material we talked about, instead of going to sleep, he got better. My brother Charles was the same way. I never saw a guy so immune to non-pertinent information as Charlesworth.

We did do crazy things to take the edge of the intense workload. One time on the Cape we had been out to eat and were leaving in our GSA car, 'grey ghost' as they were known. Grissom was there and driving his new Corvette. I challenged him to show our grey ghost what his Vette could do. We lost! When we drove back to the motel I drove the darn thing into the surf behind the motel. Tom Carter thought it was the funniest thing in the world. He was out there trying to get the door open so he could save it. Now THAT was funny.

The New Control Center in Houston

I wasn't used to the Control Center concept, i.e., working from a central location.

The new control center was to be in Houston and I was ready to come to Texas. I really never looked back. My family was from down there in fact, my Great Grandfather fought at the battle of San Jacinto. His name was John Llewellyn, and is engraved on one of monuments there.

A number of us gathered together to lay out details of the control center design. Ken Young, Charlie Parker and I and a few others sat around a table to discuss details. We got this good table and we sat there all day and we really enjoyed ourselves. I got to thinking, about how much we really didn't know, I can look at some of the group pictures from those day and think where I was, and even how I dressed then. We were really sleepwalking. It doesn't make sense how we got through it, but we had a sense of humor that you just couldn't define.

I got to thinking, every other Control Center in the world looks just like that one. It's tiered and you've got the same thing. You got the good guys, the 'diamonds' up front. You got the backup guys in the second row, then you've got all the Directors and program managers in the third row. Even a big Communications Center like Verizon and other big companies. They do the same thing. Even the Russian Control center looks like ours, and we didn't copy ours from the one we had at the Cape either.

I remember we had some plot board paper there and we sat there and said we could use that for Go, No-Go's. We developed the whole thing in the Stall and Meyers building where we had our temporary offices. We drew up all our consoles and everything on that paper. We had plot board one, the V [velocity] Gamma [flight path angle] on butcher paper with real lines drawn on it. We used that plot during the time we blew up the Atlas Agena. The Range Safety Officer (RSO) got it because it's predicted impact point was right in the middle of Houston. I'll never forget that. I tried to keep that Plot Board paper, but somebody else got it.

Soon the need to write requirements as opposed to sketching out what we wanted on butcher paper became well, a requirement. I'd get so pissed off about requirements. Everything was a requirement: you had to write it down and defend it.

Lyndon Johnson actually did a good job by putting the Control Center in Texas, because he opened up the whole state for High Tech. This new control facility had a number of "high tech" features we never had before. A new innovation for us was what was known as the "p-tube" (pneumatic canisters). Whenever we pushed a button a copy was made of our displays. That worked to help solve a tracking problem we had on GT-6.

For retro-fire we would upload the retro-fire times to the spacecraft from the CSQ tracking ship. Retro fire itself would occur shortly thereafter though out of coverage by the CSQ and prior to acquisition by the 'Range Tracker ["Rat Rack"]. Our tracking data would come through Goddard but in the case of the "Rat Rack" at Kwajalein, they didn't know precisely where the antenna was located so the vector wasn't reliable. I told them at the Naval facilities in Port Hueneme to put a submarine there and transmit their location to us. And darned if they didn't do it. That gave us the key location information we needed to get an accurate post-retro fire vector. [3]

When we saw the data on the screen we began taking a string of hard copies. That's when the front row of the control room was filled with the pneumatic tubes that looked like empty105 mm howitzer shells that filled our trenches in Korea. That's when I commented that it looked like a trench in Korea. That's when I called it the "TRENCH." The name stuck.

GT-8 was an important flight as we were to do our first docked burn with the Agena in-orbit target vehicle. One morning I had a late morning shift and when I came in I couldn't find a parking place. I didn't want to be late so I drove my Triumph up on the lawn outside the control Center. I don't know why I did it. I didn't think of anything except getting to the console. I had planned on coming back out and moving it but it was about 1 pm when my secretary called and said the guards were there. Then she said I think you'd better go now because Dr. Gilruth is there

---

3 *Wasn't long before Kraft called me up, he said "Retro, I'm sitting here with, Bob Gilruth. I've got him on and I'm not gonna' give you too much rope, because I know you'll hang yourself. But did you or did you not tell the people at Port Hueneme where the 'Rat Rack' was and to put a submarine under it?" I said, "yeah, I told them because they didn't know where it was."*

too. I did move the car but not before I got a ticket and had my parking sticker scraped off. And they wouldn't allow me another for a month! I asked the guards how was I going to get to work? And they replied they didn't care.

So I bought one of those children's bicycles with the large front wheel and two small wheels in the back and rode that through the gate. It got in everyone's way and upset the guards. Getting a ride from others wasn't working either.

By then we were about to launch GT-9. I was on the launch phase which picked up about 5 am. I had to get into the Center so I trailered my horse to a lot across the street from NASA and rode him in. The guard told me "you can't ride that [deleted] horse in here." I told him that the road into the center was designated a Texas Farm to Market road so don't tell me I can't ride my horse. In exasperation, he said "go on through." When Gene Kranz found out there was a horse now on the grass outside the Control Center he went berserk. In fact a lot of people went berserk. But I had made my point. Wasn't too long before I finally got my sticker back.

I can't remember anything about my family or home. I can't remember anything except that I was that much absorbed in my job. I think a lot of people were. I think after Apollo we finally looked around and found that we actually had children and families, you know.

Apollo, by its very complexity, was different. Those of us running full time on Gemini—we knew about it, and were interested but we didn't have time to treat it operationally.

Apollo was a lot more sophisticated. We had the on-board computer and were able to navigate and align the platform. Understanding how that worked, even though it was a lot more sophisticated than Gemini, being able to go through with Gemini as we did really helped everybody.

We had the fuel cells, that made being able to have electrical power and understand that and not have the kind of problems we had with Mercury, and the environmental control system that we had, the more flexibility with maneuverability, being able to do maneuvers that restart an engine in orbit. That's good. That's something that came out of the Gemini Program, those hypergolic fuels and stuff. The heat shield, the heat protection scheme was a lot better, a lot lighter.

By this time I had seven or eight more retrofire officers that I worked with, so we were building up that capability in anticipation of the Apollo schedule. I think, the big difference between Apollo and Gemini was that we were pretty comfortable about doing the operation with men in it and understanding how to do countdowns and how to get ready for a mission and all the pieces. We'd come up with a lot better way to make sure that we had the right information and we had a book and we had it all in one.

We had to build another real-time system. That's what flight controllers did. Interesting thing, we built our own tools just as we did when we were kids. We all improvised and built rockets or airplanes. I took an old DDT can and those things in those days, they were a big [cylindrical] canister, And you pumped them up with compressed air. I took one of those angle irons, 90 degrees and used it for my rocket sled. I greased it. We heated the cannister and with a hammer and a nail I banged it and that thing took off. I had already nearly killed myself on my bicycle by taking off the pier. I thought I was John Wayne. I waited for the tide to go down and I come down this hill with my bike that I had fastened wings to. In those days it was hard to get a bicycle. I came off that pier like a rock. It didn't even do anything. It went straight down and I ended up in the mud, cut my head and I couldn't see my bike, not even a wheel. We weren't afraid of trying and doing our own thing. So when we had to write requirements we would jump in.

I don't know how that got started, but writing the requirement for a system, and then going away and having different groups of people implementing those requirements, like the software requirements, the hardware requirements, the stuff we needed to know about the onboard systems, and, of course, the mission rules was how we did it.

The Apollo program was very complex with the number of vehicles and the pieces and the new people, and the new trajectory stuff we had to learn and build. The Return-to-Earth process was a huge development as was the determination of the trajectory parameters between the Moon and the Earth and how you did that.

We had a Lunar sphere of influence and an Earth sphere of influence. That is a two body problem but you can't have three. You can only have the Earth and the spacecraft, or the spacecraft and the Moon. You can't have all three of them in it, it's just tough to do. In fact, that's probably why they came up with quantum mechanics, because they couldn't do it otherwise.

We spent an awful lot of time getting away from Gemini and letting the guys that I had trained come along. I took on a new administrative role where I had all these new decisions to make and we spent a lot of time doing it. I mean, we'd come in on Saturdays for mission rules review and writing requirements. We worked at night and developed these real-time systems.

All of us did that. I know Glynn Lunney, Philip Shaffer, Charley Parker and Will Fenner and all those guys spent a lot of time with their new hat on, getting ready for the lunar stuff. We argued with everybody, too. It got to be—I have a feeling when people saw us coming from Building 45 or 30, they actually went out and bought a lot of chow, because they knew we were coming over and we were going to argue and holler at them and all that stuff.

And really that's what happened to the Apollo guys. I mean, as we got out of that and I went onto Skylab, I really didn't want to leave. But I left there about Apollo 13, or right after that. I still talked to the Apollo people but I really got into the Skylab, and before I knew it, I was absorbed in that and all the other things we were doing.

I really could tell somewhere, and I don't know where it was, it was probably before [Apollo] 13, that we didn't have many flights left, and I couldn't understand it. I think we realized it was coming to an end at [Apollo] 17 for some reason. Yet we had a lot of boosters left. We had the spacecraft. I felt like that we should really get in there and try to bring some stuff back, like some of that H3 and some of the stuff that we were really—you know, the things that we were trying to do, because we just scratched the surface. We knew what we were doing.

We were confident. And I think when I found that out, you know, and I knew that it was going to come to an end, and I think I changed the way I looked at things. But let's say from [19]'59 to '69, those ten years were really incredible, and then all of a sudden not to do it anymore, I think it impacted a lot of people's lives that realized that once that you've done that, then what else are you going do?

When Apollo ended, I told Kraft, "We lost the best job we ever had and we didn't do anything wrong!"

32

Made in the USA
Lexington, KY
27 May 2016